P9-EKD-912

MASTERING ORIGAMI

# PRACTICAL

# ORIGAMI

*MASTERING ORIGAMI*

# PRACTICAL
# ORIGAMI

Tom Butler and Michael G. LaFosse

**Enslow Publishing**
101 W. 23rd Street
Suite 240
New York, NY 10011
USA

enslow.com

Published in 2017 by Enslow Publishing, LLC
101 W. 23rd Street, Suite 240, New York, NY 10011

**Library of Congress Cataloging-in-Publication Data**

Names: Butler, Tom.
Title: Practical origami / Tom Butler and Michael G. LaFosse.
Description: New York : Enslow Publishing, 2017 | Series: Mastering origami | Includes bibliographical references and index.
Identifiers: ISBN 9780766079557 (pbk.) | ISBN 9780766079564 (library bound) | ISBN 9780766079595 (6 pack)
Subjects: LCSH: Origami—Juvenile literature.
Classification: LCC TT870.B885 2017 | DDC 736'.982—dc23

Printed in the United States of America

**To Our Readers:** We have done our best to make sure all website addresses in this book were active and appropriate when we went to press. However, the author and the publisher have no control over and assume no liability for the material available on those websites or on any websites they may link to. Any comments or suggestions can be sent by e-mail to customerservice@enslow.com.

**Photos Credits:** Art throughout book: windesign/Shutterstock.com (geometric background), Janos Timea/Shutterstock.com (banners), butterflycreative/Shutterstock.com (book title); origami projects by Michael G. LaFosse; photographs of projects by Adriana Skura and Cindy Reiman.

# CONTENTS

# INTRODUCTION

Origami, the Japanese art of paper folding, has been an important part of Japan's culture for more than two thousand years. In the Japanese language, *ori* means "folding" and *kami* means "paper." At first, paper folders used simple folds to bring to mind the shape of a flower, an animal, or a bird. Over time, people found many practical uses for shapes made from origami. You can make your own origami bookmarks, **greeting cards**, and gift boxes!

In Japan, children learn origami at a young age. Origami uses a language of **symbols**, just like music. Once you know origami symbols, you can read an origami book from anywhere in the world. Use the key on pages 8 and 9 to help you make your origami projects. The key explains terms such as *mountain fold* and *valley fold* and shows you the different symbols that are used throughout the book.

Most of the origami projects in this book are made from square-shaped paper. Most origami paper has color on only one side, but you do not need to buy special origami paper. You can make origami using gift-wrapping paper, old magazines, colorful notepapers, even candy wrappers! Just be sure the paper you use

is square. It also must be the right size for the project you are making. When you start a project, make sure the paper faces in the same way as it does in the instructions.

Some origami projects need more than one sheet of paper. There are **several** of these designs in this book. By combining several folded shapes, you can make many kinds of projects. As you fold, look ahead at the next instruction to see what the paper's shape will look like. This will help you better understand how the symbols and drawings work together. Once you are familiar with the folds, you can start to invent your own practical origami creations!

# ORIGAMI FOLDS AND SYMBOLS

## 1. MOUNTAIN FOLD

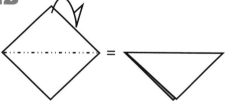

MOUNTAIN FOLD LINE

To make a mountain fold, hold the paper so the bottom (white) side is facing up. Fold the top corner back (away from you) to meet the bottom corner.

## 2. VALLEY FOLD

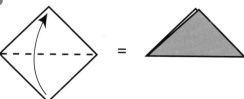

VALLEY FOLD LINE

To make a valley fold, hold the paper so the white side is facing up. Fold the bottom corner up to meet the top corner.

## 3. ROTATE

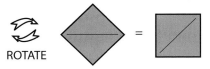

ROTATE

## 6. CUT

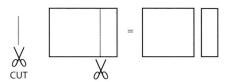

CUT    CUT

## 4. TURN OVER

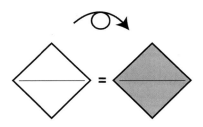

## 7. FOLD AND UNFOLD

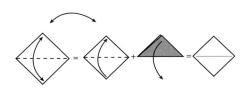

## 5. MOVE OR PUSH

MOVE or PUSH

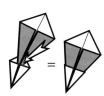

## 8. DIRECTION ARROW

# BOOKMARK

A bookmark is an object that you put in your book to hold your place. This origami bookmark holds your place. It also tells you which side of the page you were on! Because of the folds, it stays in place and does not fall out like other bookmarks sometimes do. You can make bookmarks for your family, teachers, and friends. Even better, you can teach them how to make bookmarks.

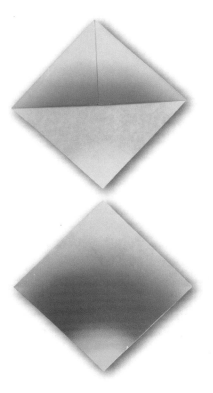

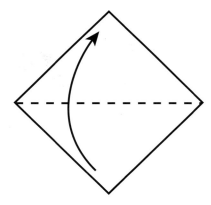

**1.** Use a square piece of paper 6 inches (15.2 cm) wide or less. If you are using origami paper, begin with the white side up. Fold the bottom corner to the top corner to make a triangle.

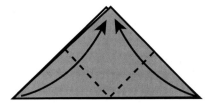

**2.** Making clean creases, fold the two bottom corners to the top.

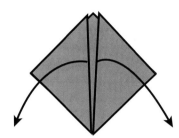

**3.** Bring the two corners back down and make a triangle again.

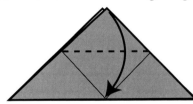

**4.** Fold down the top corner.

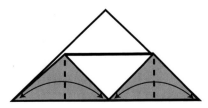

**5.** Fold the two bottom corners so that they meet. Unfold them again.

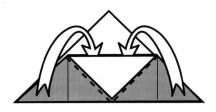

**6.** Fold the two triangles on the bottom left and right corners up and over the folded white triangle. Push the two corners inside the paper, behind the white triangle.

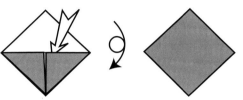

**7.** You have one of the world's greatest bookmarks! You can decorate the bookmark any way you like!

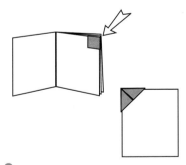

**8.** Place the bookmark in a page of this book. See how well this bookmark fits? Place the large square side of the bookmark on the page you are reading. If you open the book to the back side of the bookmark, you will know that you were not reading this page.

# STAR FRAME

A frame surrounds a picture on all sides. Frames allow us to handle a photo, drawing, or other picture without damaging it. Frames can also make the picture within it look better. Frames help people look at the picture and see it more clearly. An origami frame is a handmade frame that is also a work of art. You can frame a special picture with your own origami frame made from folded paper.

You can use any type of square paper for this project. The bigger the picture is, the bigger the frame needs to be. The bigger the frame is, the bigger the paper needs to be.

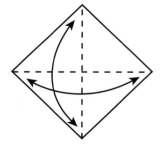

1. Begin with a square piece of paper. If you are using origami paper, start with the white side up. Fold the paper in half, from one corner to the other corner, to make a triangle. Open the paper and fold it in half the other way. See how the creases are crossed in the middle of the paper?

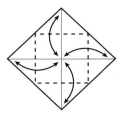

**2.** Neatly fold each corner of the square toward the center where the creases cross. Now unfold the corners. Look at the new creases you made. They make a square. Each new crease should cross one of the creases from Step 1.

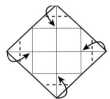 

**3.** Fold each corner of the square to touch the closest line in front of it. Now fold the folded edges again. This will make a frame shape. The folds to do this are already in your paper. You made them in Step 2!

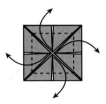

**4.** You can use this simple frame for a photograph or a picture. You can make a frame any size you want by using bigger or smaller paper. For an even prettier frame, follow the next steps to make a star frame.

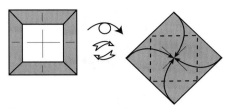

**5.** Turn your frame over and rotate it. Fold each of the four corners toward the center where the lines cross.

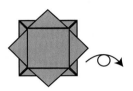

**6.** Take each corner from the middle of the paper and fold it out. You have made an eight-pointed star!

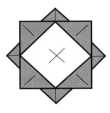

**7.** Turn over the paper. Now you have an eight-pointed star frame. You can put pictures in this frame and either keep it for yourself or give it as a gift.

# GIFT BOW

Make any gift more special with a hand-folded bow. This origami bow stands out like a shining star, especially if you use shiny paper. You can use any kind of paper to make these bows. They are a good way to **recycle** leftover scraps of wrapping paper. Just cut the scraps into squares and make as many bows as you like. You can match the paper that you used to wrap the gift or choose a color that contrasts with it.

These bows have a lot of folds, but they are quick and easy to make. Use large squares to make big bows for big packages and small squares to make little bows for little packages.

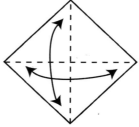

1. Use a square piece of paper 8 inches (20.3 cm) wide or less. If you are using wrapping paper or origami paper, start with the white side up. Fold in half each way corner to corner, to make crossing creases. Unfold.

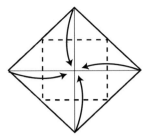

**2.** Fold in all four corners to meet in the middle.

**3.** Fold the four new corners to the middle.

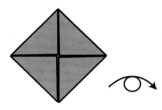

**4.** Turn the paper over.

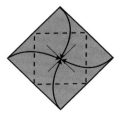

**5.** Fold the four corners to the middle again.

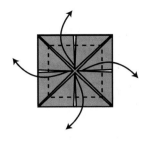

**6.** Neatly fold a little of each corner to make an eight-pointed star.

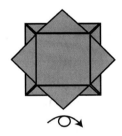

**7.** Turn the paper over.

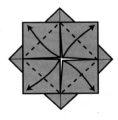

**8.** Fold the middle corners out to open the bow. You should have eight points in the middle of the bow.

# HOLIDAY WREATH

This elegant origami wreath is a great holiday decoration to put on your front door or in your window. You can also make smaller wreaths to put on a table as part of a **centerpiece** or to use as **place cards** for guests at a holiday dinner.

Make this wreath using one or two colors. This wreath is a bit like a puzzle with many pieces. You will need ten pieces of paper to complete this project. Use glue to help hold the wreath together. Use colors that reflect the season or the holiday.

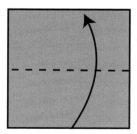

1. Use a square piece of paper 6 inches (15.2 cm) wide or less. If you are using wrapping paper or origami paper, start with the colored side up. Fold it in half, bottom edge to top.

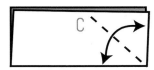

**2.** Carefully fold down the right-side short edge of paper to line up with the bottom edge. Unfold.

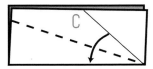

**3.** Neatly line up the C crease with the bottom edge.

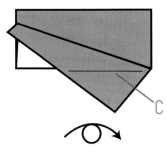

**4.** Turn the paper over, left to right.

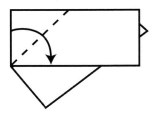

**5.** Fold the short, left edge down and line it up with the long, folded edge.

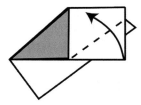

**6.** Fold up the right corner. This is the pocket.

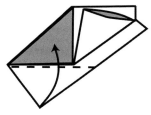

**7.** Fold up the bottom corner. Now you have a finished "leaf" for your wreath.

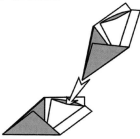

**8.** Make nine more pieces like this, and fit each pointed end into a pocket.

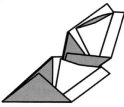

**9.** The pieces should fit together to look like the picture above.

# POCKET CARD

A greeting card can be as simple as a folded sheet of paper. Most cards are folded so that a personal message can be written on the inside. Before there were machine-made papers and modern **printing presses**, greeting cards were handmade. Today most greeting cards are made by machine. This is why a handmade card is so special. You can make it even more special by decorating the card.

This card is made with pockets. You can put a secret note, stickers, a piece of candy, or even movie tickets inside the pockets. You can decorate the outside pocket by gluing on an origami flower, sunburst, or other shape.

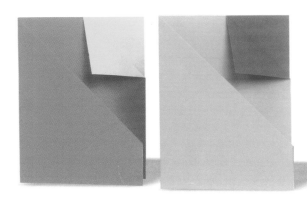

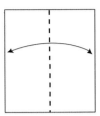

1. Use paper that measures 8 ½ inches (21.6 cm) by 11 inches (27.9 cm). Valley fold the paper in half lengthwise. Unfold. You have made a center crease line.

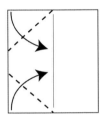

2. Valley fold the top and bottom corners on the left side to the crease line.

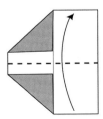

3. Valley fold the paper in half along dotted lines.

4. Valley fold the paper in half from left to right.

5. Valley fold down the top corner to make the point touch the folded edges of the front layers.

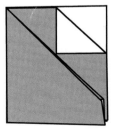

6. The finished card is now ready to decorate!

# VALENTINE'S DAY CARD

The heart shape stands for love in many countries. Giving someone an origami heart card is a special way to wish that person a happy Valentine's Day. You can also give cards decorated with hearts for other **occasions** such as birthdays, Mother's Day, and Father's Day. If you love someone, tell him or her often and in different ways. You can send someone you love a card with this origami heart design. Make several of these hearts and place them inside a pocket card. Or glue an origami heart on a blank card and write "I love you" on top of the heart.

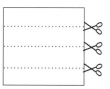

1. Use 6-inch (15.2 cm) square paper. Fold the paper into four equal parts and unfold. Cut the paper along the creases. You just made four equal-sized rectangles. These four rectangles will be used to make four hearts.

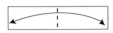

**2.** Valley fold one of the rectangles in half. Unfold.

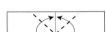

**3.** Valley fold the bottom left and the bottom right edges to make them meet at the center crease.

**4.** Turn the paper facedown.

**5.** Valley fold down the top edges to match them to the edge of paper across the middle.

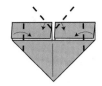

**6.** Fold down the two corners at the top center of the split. Valley fold the left and right edges, about a third of the distance to the center.

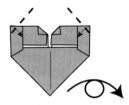

**7.** Valley fold down the corners at the top outside of the heart. Turn the paper over.

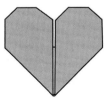

**8.** Use the card to decorate a plain card or the pocket card you made in the previous project.

# BIRTHDAY CARD

Origami flower cards are bright and cheerful. Give these cards to celebrate birthdays. They can also be used to celebrate other holidays, such as Mother's Day, or as a gift for someone who loves flowers.

Flowers grow in many different colors. You can choose the color of your origami flower based on the holiday or the season. Make red, white, and green origami flowers to decorate cards you will give during the winter. Orange and gold flowers are ideal for autumn. In the spring, make your origami flowers with soft pastel-colored papers. Red and purple flowers can be used in the summer. You can make these origami flowers quickly and in any size. You can also try different folds on the petals.

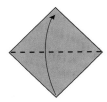

**1.** Use two 6-inch (15.2 cm) square papers. One of the papers should be green. The other can be any color you choose. Take the paper that is not green and valley fold it in half, bottom corner to top corner.

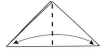

**2.** Valley fold the paper in half again, corner to corner. Unfold to make a center crease.

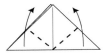

**3.** Valley fold up the two side corners toward the top corner. Corners should not be folded to meet at the center crease line, otherwise you will make a diamond shape. Look at Step 4 to see how the shape should appear.

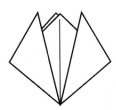

**4.** This is a basic flower shape. Next, take the green colored paper and repeat Steps 1 through 3. This is the stem of the flower.

**5.** Mountain fold the sides of the stem around to the back. This will make the stem narrower than the flower. Push the flower into the top of the stem, between the two layers of the center corner.

**6.** This is the finished flower to put on the card. Try to shape the petals of the flower differently and see what other kinds of flowers you can create!

# CHRISTMAS CARD

This clever Christmas tree card is made up of three origami plant shapes. Trees and plants are helpful to people. They produce oxygen. Oxygen is a gas that has no color, taste, or smell. People and animals need it to live. Plants are symbols of growth, food, and strength.

Throughout history, trees and plants that stay green all year have had special meaning for people in the winter. They reminded people that plants would grow again when summer returned. It is believed that German Christians began the tradition of bringing decorated trees inside to celebrate Christmas. Use your imagination to think of what else you can make with this **classic** origami plant shape.

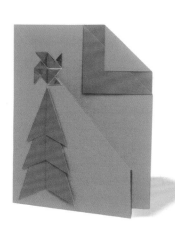

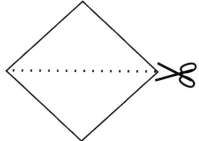

**1.** Use 6-inch (15.2 cm) square paper. Valley fold in half, corner to corner. Unfold. Cut along the crease lines as shown to make two triangles.

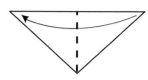

**2.** Valley fold in half, corner to corner.

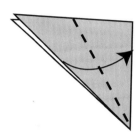

**3.** Position the triangle so that the folded edge is facing right. Hold the top layer and valley fold to meet the folded edge.

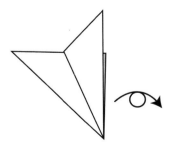

**4.** Turn the paper facedown.

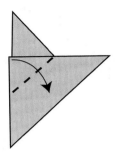

**5.** The paper will have one large triangle and a smaller one. Valley fold the left corner of the large triangle over to lock the layers together.

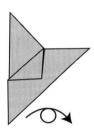

**6.** Turn the paper over.

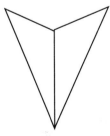

**7.** This is the finished shape. Use three of these shapes to form a Christmas tree. Glue the tree onto the front of a card.

# HALLOWEEN CARD

**B**ased on an Irish folktale about a man named Stingy Jack, the jack-o'-lantern is one of the most popular symbols of Halloween. Pumpkin origami cards are great to send to friends. Choose bright orange paper for your origami jack-o'-lantern. Then decorate it with your favorite jack-o'-lantern expression! Use your imagination. Does your pumpkin grin, frown, or snarl? Is it scary, friendly, or just plain goofy? Use your origami jack-o'-lanterns as Halloween decorations or as invitations to a Halloween party. Have an origami-folding contest at your party. See who can fold an origami jack-o'-lantern the fastest!

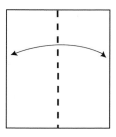

1. Use paper that is 8 ½ inches (21.6 cm) by 11 inches (27.9 cm). Valley fold it lengthwise. Unfold it to create a center crease.

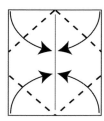

2. Carefully valley fold all four corners to the center crease. Look at the next step to see how your shape should look.

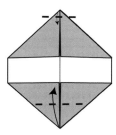

3. Valley fold the bottom corner so that it meets the base of the triangle at the center crease. Fold down the top corner a little bit to make it flat.

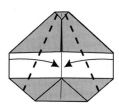

4. Valley fold the sides to meet in the middle. It should look like the shape below.

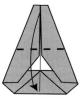

5. Valley fold in half, top to bottom.

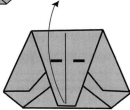

6. Valley fold up part of the top flap of paper to make the stem.

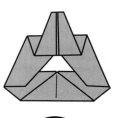

7. Turn it over. Look at the photograph on the opposite page to see how it should look. Draw a face on your pumpkin and turn it into a jack-o'-lantern!

# ORIGAMI PINWHEEL CARD

The pinwheel is a classic children's toy. It is made of brightly colored paper or plastic curls attached in the center by a pin to a stick. Toy pinwheels spin in the wind or when you blow on them. They have delighted children for hundreds of years.

An origami pinwheel is a fun card decoration for celebrations such as New Year's Eve, Independence Day, and birthdays. Choose colorful paper and make several origami pinwheels. Try different ways to arrange your pinwheels.

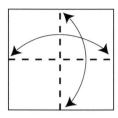

**1.** Use 6-inch (15.2 cm) square paper. Valley fold in half lengthwise. Unfold. Valley fold in half again from top to bottom. Unfold. You will have four squares.

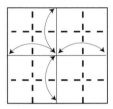

**2.** One at a time, valley fold and unfold each of the four edges to the center creases.

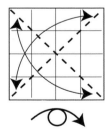

**3.** Valley fold in half, corner to corner, both ways. Unfold and turn the paper over.

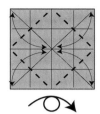

**4.** Valley fold each of the four corners to meet at the center. Unfold and turn the paper over.

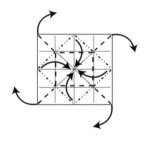

**5.** Using the creases that you made, move the middle edges of the square to the center while valley folding the corners in half. Make the pinwheel shape by mountain folding each corner down in a clockwise direction.

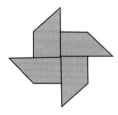

**6.** Your finished pinwheel should look like this. Make pinwheels in different colors to decorate your card.

# ORIGAMI PINEAPPLE CARD

Italian **explorer** Christopher Columbus brought pineapples back to Europe from his travels to the Caribbean. Pineapples were a rare treat in Europe. Only wealthy people could afford to buy them. The display of a pineapple at the dinner table showed guests that they were invited to a special meal and that they were **honored**. This was how the pineapple came to stand for **hospitality**. Give pineapple cards to welcome a new classmate or new neighbors. Origami pineapples also make cheerful baby shower cards to welcome the arrival of a new baby!

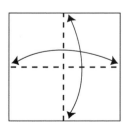

**1.** Use 6-inch (15.2 cm) square paper. Valley fold in half, lengthwise. Unfold. Fold in half top to bottom. Unfold.

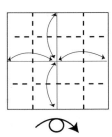

**2.** One at a time, valley fold and unfold each of the four edges to the center creases. Turn the paper facedown.

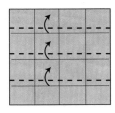

**3.** One at a time, fold each of the three horizontal creases so that they overlap a little of the paper above them.

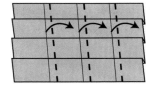

**4.** One at a time, grab each of the three vertical creases and valley fold them to the right, overlapping the paper.

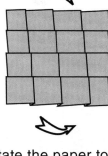

**5.** Rotate the paper to the diagonal position shown in Step 6.

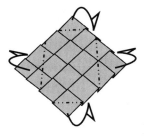

**6.** Mountain fold the four corners around to the back to make the pineapple shape.

**7.** Make one origami plant (from pages 24–25) and add it to the back of the pineapple. Glue both onto a card.

# FORTUNE COOKIE PUZZLE BOX

This clever puzzle box looks like a Chinese fortune cookie. You can use it hold little gifts or as a holiday ornament. These boxes are especially pretty when folded from colorful squares of wrapping paper. To make an extra-sturdy box, use squares of leftover wallpaper. Extra folds in this box help display the colors on the corners. You can make tiny boxes and use them as beads. Each box has a small hole through which you can pass a thread. After you string the boxes, you can wear them around your neck like a necklace. Once you learn how to fold this box, you will find them quick and easy to make.

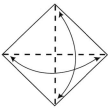

**1.** Use three 10-inch- (25.4-cm-) square papers. Position the paper so that it is diamond shaped. Valley fold it in half, in both directions, and unfold it.

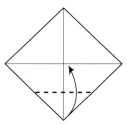

**2.** Valley fold up the bottom corner point to touch the center of the paper.

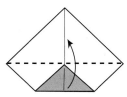

**3.** Fold up the bottom edge to the center of the paper. Use the dotted line as a guide.

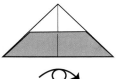

**4.** Your paper will look like this. Turn the paper over.

**5.** Fold the paper in half, right corner to left corner. Unfold it. Next fold up the left and the right corners to the top corner. Look at Step 6 to see how the paper should appear.

X 3

**6.** Unfold the left and right corners that you made in the last step. Repeat these steps for the rest of the papers.

Outside View

Pockets

Tabs

**7.** The outside of each puzzle piece has mountain creases and two pockets. The half-square corners are the tabs.

**8.** Slip both tabs of one puzzle piece into the pocket of another. Add the third piece the same way. All of the valley creases face inside the box.

# FOX BOX

You can use this clever little box in many ways. It is a gift box, a puzzle, a bead, or a fortune cookie! Larger paper squares make larger boxes and tiny paper squares make tiny boxes. See how small a box you can make. The smallest boxes can be strung together like beads to wear as a necklace or to use as a decoration. Add a piece of candy and a note to a fox box and you have a paper fortune cookie. The folded papers look like three little fox heads, so this design is named the fox box.

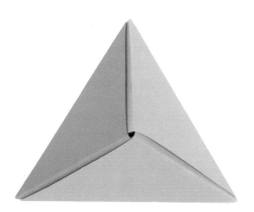

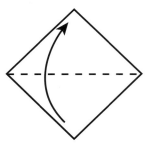

1. Use three square pieces of paper 6 inches (15.2 cm) wide or less. If you are using origami paper, begin with the white side up. Fold the bottom corner to the top corner to make a colored triangle.

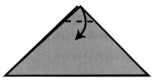

**2.** Fold down a small part of the top front corner. This will be the fox's nose.

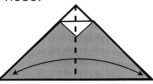

**3.** Fold the triangle in half. Then unfold.

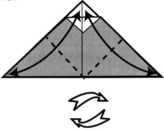

**4.** Fold the two bottom corners to the top square corner.

**5.** Unfold and rotate the paper so that the "nose" is at the bottom. Do you see the tall, pointy ears and the triangular face? Do you see how the fox's mouth opens under his nose? If you make three fox heads, you can build a fox box.

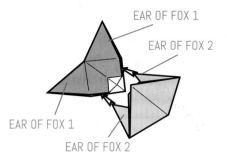

EAR OF FOX 1
EAR OF FOX 2
EAR OF FOX 1
EAR OF FOX 2

**6.** To make a fox box, remember that "ears go into mouths." Each fox box will eat both ears of the other fox. Fit two foxes together by pushing both ears of fox #2 into the mouth of fox #1.

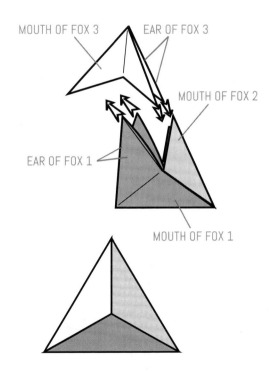

MOUTH OF FOX 3   EAR OF FOX 3
MOUTH OF FOX 2
EAR OF FOX 1
MOUTH OF FOX 1

**7.** Add fox #3 by pushing its ears into the mouth of fox #2.

# MASU BOX

**A**masu is a traditional Japanese wooden box used to measure beans, rice, and other grains. This masu box will be made with paper and can be used to store things. Use small masu boxes to hold hair clips, coins, or other small treasures. Use large masu boxes to store supplies, toys, or other items.

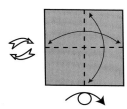

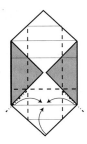

**1.** Use an 8 1/2-inch (21.6 cm) square paper. Valley fold it in half, edge to edge, each way. Unfold it after each fold. Turn the paper over, and rotate it.

**5.** Make the box walls by valley folding up the left and the right sides and then the bottom edge. Use the creases to bring in the bottom edge. Use the creases to bring in the bottom corners. Look ahead at Step 6 for the shape.

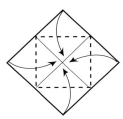

**2.** Valley fold all four corners to the center.

**6.** Valley fold the bottom corner. The paper point will go inside, to the bottom of the box.

**3.** Valley fold each edge of the square to the center, then unfold the paper.

**7.** Do Step 6 on the top

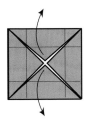

**4.** Open the top and the bottom corners

**8.** Your finished masu box should look like this.

# SKULL MASK

Many countries pay respect to the dead. In Mexico, a holiday called the Day of the Dead is **observed** on November 1 and 2. It is a time to honor family members who have died. It is not a sad time but rather a joyful one. Families celebrate Day of the Dead with flowers, food, and parades. They visit the graves of their **ancestors**. Human skeletons and skulls are common symbols of this Mexican holiday. Mexicans make candies and pastries in the shapes of skulls. They wear or display skull masks. You can use this skull mask to celebrate Day of the Dead. You can also use it as part of a Halloween costume.

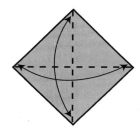

1. Use a 10-inch (25.4 cm) square paper. Fold and unfold from top to bottom and from side to side.

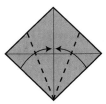

**2.** Fold the bottom two edges to meet at the center crease line to make a kite shape.

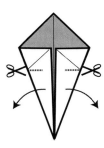

**3.** Cut two slits, one on each side, at the level where the creases touch the folded edges of the paper. Unfold this kite shape.

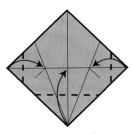

**4.** Fold up the bottom corner to touch the center of the paper, where the creases cross. Fold in the left and the right corners to the place where the slits meet the crease line.

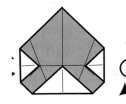

**5.** Turn the paper over and rotate it as shown.

**6.** Open the eyes by folding up the cut edges of paper. Mountain and valley fold the bottom corner to make the teeth.

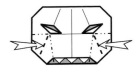

**7.** Using the crease marks, mountain and valley fold the sides of the skull to make the jaw narrow. Push in the sides of the skull as shown.

**8.** Make the skull mask less flat by adding these mountain folds and valley folds.

# MARDI GRAS MASK

**M**ardi Gras is French for "fat Tuesday." For some Christians, Mardi Gras is the last chance to celebrate before Lent. Lent is the period of forty days before Easter during which many Christians give up something they enjoy. Many Christians see Lent as a time of **spiritual renewal** and **fasting**. Mardi Gras is a time for fun, food, and festivities! People often dress in costumes and wear masks to parties and parades during Mardi Gras. The traditional Mardi Gras mask hides only the upper part of your face. That way, you are free to laugh, smile, talk, and eat.

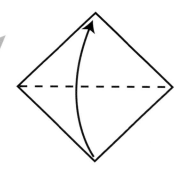

**1.** Use 8-inch (20.3 cm) square paper. Valley fold in half, bottom corner to top corner.

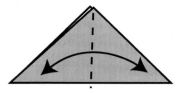

**2.** Valley fold the paper in half, from the left corner to the right corner. Unfold the paper.

**3.** Valley fold up the left and the right corners to match up to the top corner.

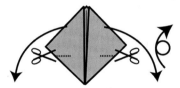

**4.** Cut a slit on both the left and the right sides of the folded edges. Notice that the cuts are made below the left and right corners. Unfold the top two corners. Turn the paper upside down.

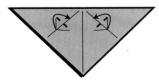

**5.** Open the eye holes by folding up the two cut corners.

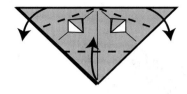

**6.** Valley fold up the bottom corner, but not so high as to cover the eyes. Valley fold down the two top corners. Be sure that they make a wide shape.

**7.** Valley fold up the two corners to make the two horns.

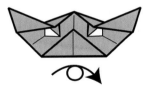

**8.** Turn the paper over.

**9.** Mountain crease the center of the mask. Valley fold the creases that line up with the eye holes.

# KITE STAR

This simple shape, the kite, can be used to make stars of all shapes and sizes. You can glue these stars to the front of a card, write notes on the back and give them as gifts, or use them to decorate the walls or ceiling in your room. Once you learn how to make the basic shape, you will be able to invent new projects of your own. Use paper with different colors, patterns, and textures to add even more variety.

You will need four sheets of square paper to make the basic kite star. The four squares for each star must be the same size. You also will need clear tape.

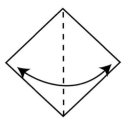

**1.** Begin with one piece of square paper. If you are using origami paper, start with the white side up. Fold the paper in half, from one corner to the other corner, to make a triangle shape. Now unfold.

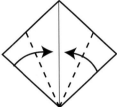

**2.** Fold the two bottom edges to the crease line at the middle of the paper.

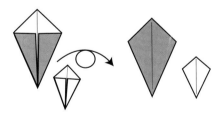

**3.** Now you have a kite shape! You can make big kites or small kites by using different sizes of square paper. Turn the kite over to see the display, or colorful, side of this origami shape. Now make three more. You need four same-size kites to make a kite star.

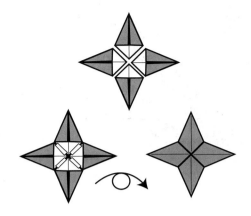

**4.** On the back, tape the four origami kites together to make one star. Turn over the taped papers to see your beautiful star.

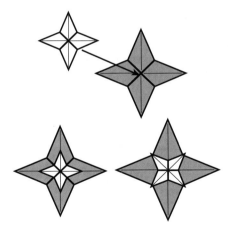

**5.** Repeat Steps 1 through 4 using four smaller pieces of different colored paper. Turn the small star to match the same position as the larger star or rotate it so that the points are between the points of the larger star.

# SUNBURST

**B**ecause this origami form looks like a brilliant sun, we call it a sunburst. Use this starburst to brighten a window, decorate a greeting card, or give as a gift.

This project is like the kite star. If you have made a kite star, you can make this sunburst. You will need a total of twenty-four pieces of square paper. You need eight squares for the large kites, eight squares (half the size of the paper for the large kites) for the small kites, and eight squares (the same size as the large kite papers) for the diamonds. Use three different colors of paper to get the best effect. Use clear tape to hold the finished pieces together.

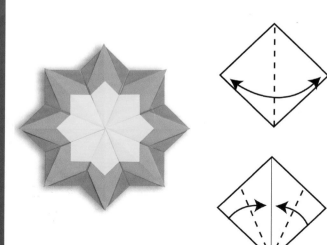

**1.** To make a large kite, begin with one piece of square paper. If you are using origami paper, start with the white side up. Fold the paper in half, from one corner to the other corner, and then unfold.

**2.** Fold the two bottom edges to the crease line at the middle of the paper.

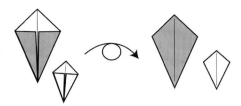

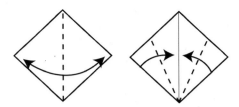

**3.** Now you have the kite shape! Make seven more kite shapes by repeating Steps 1 and 2 seven more times. You can make big kites or small kites by using different sizes of square paper. Now make eight small kites the same way by using a different color of paper.

**6.** Use eight pieces of the same size square paper that you used to make your large kites. However, use a different color of paper. Fold the paper in half, from one corner to the other corner, and then unfold. Fold the bottom edges to the crease line in the middle of the paper. This is just like making a kite.

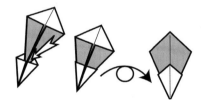

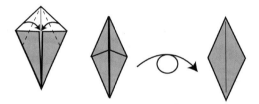

**4.** See how a large kite fits into a small kite? Turn the kites over to see the beautiful pattern. Put your eight large kites and your eight small kites together to build a sunburst.

**7.** Fold the top, short edges of the kite to the middle to make a diamond shape. All four sides on this new diamond should be equal. Make seven more diamonds.

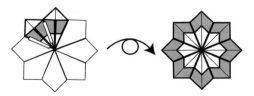

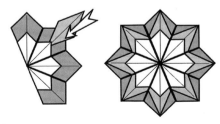

**5.** Tape the kites together on the backside and turn the paper over to see the beautiful design.

**8.** Push the eight diamonds into the top of the eight small kites.

# GLOSSARY

**ancestor**—A person from whom another person is descended.

**centerpiece**— A decorative display put in the center of a table.

**classic**—Something that is known as being the best or typical of its kind.

**explorer**—A person who travels in search of new land or scientific information.

**fasting**—To go without eating.

**greeting card**—A decorated card with a message for another person that is usually sent on a special occasion.

**honor**—To show great respect for.

**hospitality**—The friendly and generous treatment of visitors and guests.

**observe**—To celebrate with special events or customs.

**occasion**—A special day, event, or ceremony.

**place card**—A card featuring a guest's name that is used to indicate where that guest should sit at the dinner table.

**printing press**—A machine that produces printed copies of works, such as books, fliers, and cards.

**recycle**—The process of reusing materials such as paper, glass, or metal.

**several**—More than two but not very many.

**spiritual renewal**—A feeling of being born again or growing in a religious sense.

**symbol**—Something that stands for something else.

# FURTHER READING

Ard, Catherine. *Origami Holidays.* New York: Gareth Stevens Publishing, 2016.

Gardiner, Matthew. *Origami Boxes.* New York: PowerKids Press, 2016.

Gardiner, Matthew. *Origami Decorations and Flowers.* New York: PowerKids Press, 2016.

Kuskowski, Alex. *Japanese Art.* Minneapolis, MN: Abdo Publishing, 2015.

# INDEX